a book of sounds

Also by Billy Mills

Genesis and Home
Triple Helix
Letters from Barcelona
Five Easy Pieces
The Properties of Stone
Tiny Pieces
A Small Book of Songs
What is a Mountain?
Logical Fallacies
Lares / Manes: Collected Poems
Imaginary Gardens
Loop Walks
The City Itself

a book of sounds

Billy Mills

Shearsman Books

First published in the United Kingdom in 2024 by
Shearsman Books
P.O. Box 4239
Swindon
SN3 9FN

Shearsman Books Ltd Registered Office
30–31 St. James Place, Mangotsfield, Bristol BS16 9JB
(this address not for correspondence)

www.shearsman.com

ISBN 978-1-84861-928-9

Copyright © Billy Mills, 2024

The right of Billy Mills to be identified as the author of this work has been asserted by him in accordance with the Copyrights, Designs and Patents Act of 1988.
All rights reserved.

i.m. Maurice Scully

FOUR

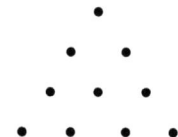

•

news for you
    stag tongues
winter snows
    summer's gone

wind high-cold
    low sun
short course
    tide's run

deep-red bracken's
    hidden form
brent geese
    cry's norm

cold's caught
    bird's wing
ice time
    that's my song

we live in water
and it in us
pellucid both
the very air

floats all near
this locus
which is here
counting strokes

the wind settles
ice in the air
patterns grass
white & crisp

fluid as stone
the light lowers
as day dies
stillness settles

a dust of leaves
under the slime
mouldering
bare as life

dormant stars
fitful
a north wind
grips us

& we sleep
uneasily

nothing in mind
that does not first

chill the flesh
the senses raw
breath suspended
sodden again

in the river a rock
in the rock a river
ice at times
at times not

death has no hold
life persists
the cold rhythm
slowly flows

turning inward

earth absorbs
that which is given
arc opens

these small changes
first rain   then ice
then thaw   then rain
earth turned water

a brown leaf floats
under the bridge
(river in spate)
slowly turning

a late stray leaf
moving onwards
& swept around
wind drives water

(current of sorts)
through chilling air
& breaks against
this house flows down

we wake to noise
& it is winter
does what it does
let the air freeze

& the earth freeze
& the water
this long night
all we have broken

in all we have made
is everything
rain constant
a time of shadows

nothing endures but
a leaf awaiting
as the bud waits
this is a line

walk it it moves
away the leaf

awaits the bud
in latency

. .

one small bird
whose note's heard
sharply pointed
      yellowbill

whose notes fly
on Loch Laig
blackbird's branch
      yellowfilled

the buds signal
& sugars rise
plane of each leaf
opens slowly

unfolding its curved
surface to air
& dawn
ever earlier

& vivid with
life erupting
listen: it is
sun on the grass

crisp & flat
'with all her hues'
that moment between
shower & shower

when nothing happens
but life itself
stirring the green
this sudden spring

sap flows
answer ascending
ask what it is
light eases through

the surface of things
as they awaken

as they arise
imperceptible heat

not heat but not
its absence
a softening
slowly thawing

earth   water   air
of which it is
the time not yet
the third is this

new surface stirring
tentative & alive
a mould supports
air's burden

which is one

& many streams
converge the oak
draws in

that which it needs
is what it will
an aura defined
by light embodied

this morning low
glow cloud around
the far plane
glimmers everything

breathes again
blackbird sings
high in the trees
each to its

other catch then
now wind from
the east chills
incipient life

itself becomes
& is contra-
distinction skim
the skin of things

stretched fine
& breathing light
suffused flat just
as day breaks again

face it feel
the grain of air
refract the early
beam of life

ascending spring
it is now
softly smooth
it spreads itself

pushing through
earth's meniscus
breaking green
the vivid air

•••

bird in the willow sings
clean tones: small bill
      beak yellow: black form
      vivace: bird's song

that it is deep
the leaf breathes
in its own way
this unifying fire

that drives all
that flows
burns gloriously
(as it should)

in memory
as much as now
the path climbs
& we follow

this bright arc
the heart stills
enter the depth
of things

& everything burns
everything sit
in this dome
of vivid tree

teeming with light
a system potent
forms the leaves
shape space

& glow a prism
 walk in the process

of respiration
a transfer south

we turn the earth
follows everything
folds outwards
opens a volume

consumed flame
serves the sun's zenith
leaves sessile
above

this oak the sky
above the sky
radiant space
uncomprehending

& below the bark
buds wait (not
willed) links
in a ring of

moments this third
is depth feel it
grow follow the sun's
arc breathe light

blow the wind
thiswards ever
a cycle drift
thermal currents

lift far power
drives the function
there is no mystery
but this fruit forms

this wave shapes
what is life a leaf
converting energy
into green deeps

the earth turns
on an axis of fire
hidden betimes
blazing again

transferring energy
a crystal lattice
the space between
weaving life

in three dimensions
light burns &
this needle turns
following sun's

trajectory brings
warm air home
leaf radiates
what it is to be

what it was again
this volume holds

its own form
its own flame

••••

three live things that shed dead things:

a deer its horns
a tree its leaves
a cow its coat

the year draws down
a gathering in
& what is gathered
shapes what follows

the earth gives
& the earth gathers
that which is given
hyphae & worms

woodlice & rain
the earth regenerates
a community
in a fallen leaf

a chestnut husk
softly browning
silver trails slick
on sparse grass

the earth renews
from this detritus
which is a process
(part of the process)

smallest composite
a number to hold
waxing crescent
above the cloud

sunset behind
& sea in the gaps
engines drone
a dried leaf

curls in on itself
in abscission
falling suddenly
& slow

cobweb traces
against the wall
blown in time
in evening sun

a pinnate net
of dried channels
resilient & lost
the earth takes

time slows life
slows the last leaves
curl so that
here the light

rises the earth
glows
in fecundity
sleep incipient

a gold-brown ground
& she who rests
& he who rests
& everything winds

the sun declines
these shorter hours
turn to them
to the western sky

oak filled with song
the migrants issue
obeying instinct
gather again

sheaves of sound
ripe in season
a great red moon
low in the west

measure the hour
under the tree
bare as it is
a single bird

grubbing for worms
a blackbird
song comes
from nowhere

& returns
nothing is lost
nothing is saved
under the leaves

we live in earth
and it in us
reconstituting
made over

Uncertain Songs

the car in the street
is a car

the street
is a street

the impression of motion
is created
by motion

all things being equal

as they never are

what might be
what is
words corrupted

everything shifts
that is
everything

light
as air
is air

an imperfection

making a sound making
a mark on a sheet
the sheet in a book
a book of sounds

listen: nothing happens
& it is good the line
bends here   here breaks

& it is good what does
it mean   not much
but everything onwards
on words

can you see how it is
the green & grey a colony
living on air   on water

on light itself radiant still
behind us the lichen is
a system of cooperation

the world is many & simple
in its complexity
& delicate oh so delicate

which is its strength & we
are not the thing itself
not what we think ourselves

these are the facts
& these are the facts
& the facts are

that we do not hold
the ice cracks & the water
which the future holds
over & the earth is
indifferent   in the end

there is no end
only the facts
we do not hold

there are these things
& we live in them   in this time
we cannot see it
will not see it
the water rises a slow weight
shifts the power of it
a robin in the mud
leaving no tracks

wind again night again
an absence of stillness
over the deep nothing moving

these walls groan   no
make a sound like the sound
of groaning no more things can be

added no more away
a point of stasis achieved
despite itself

ice makes
patterns
on the car

meaning
a robin sings
this early spring

sun cold
sings territory
what might endure

the ice holds
the morning sings
the bird

there are whispers
of beauty
in the air

which freezes over
(sing it)

somewhere
a child starves
a mother holds

& we are lost
in this death

& this air
cannot
sustain

a robin builds
driven
by need
fragile as steel

worrying at words
the bird
hesitates
or so it seems

wrong again
it is
persistent
sings

if you can at all   go outside and look at the moon

air crisp   night cold   sky clear

nobody put it there

nobody owns it

no one can sell it to you

it simply is   which is its value

paths turn back on themselves
in formal patterns
of movement & stillness
a park refinding its purpose
in people   in use
in being shared   a space
unencumbered

look

it is life these moments
outside the flow of living
things done for the doing
on a path to nowhere

because the world is broken
because we broke it
unthinkingly
& let the light flow in

there is too much light
& we are blinded
to the cracks
that we have made
unthinkingly

& cannot adjust
cannot return

opening the way
is not
it is difficult

the touch
of sun on skin
rain on skin

the gestation
not the doing

in the heat
of summer
to remember
the fall of words
the slow descent
of signs

a seagull
in the street
a new element

lost & assured
& just a little
ridiculous

start again each day anew
the thing most missed
is a place to stand

there is a morning
see it does not rise
 but we have no word

for what happens next
or then as it happens
starting again afresh

as rain as it sounds
as it falls hard against
the turning world

that the wind
that the rain
that the summer
changing

that all of this
is of our doing
& not

& that we are not
all of this
that we would be

'speaking is difficult' &
writing is worse is work
on 'the appearance of things'
which is a surface
which is itself
unspoken

drift in the light of
language which is more
than words which is
a system of difficulties
which we live in
mostly

& the world indifferent
& large evades us
which is as it is
& all we have is this
difficult & silent
speech

what is the sound of words on the page
the sound of rain unheard birds
in an imagined tree silent as speech
the mind unfolds in measure

is inexplicably the world wants nothing
happening slowly which is the sound of words
in the air distinct against us
small point in a long sentence

articulate floats marks relations
as even as language in time rolls out
on to this line silent as thought
which is a moment engaged

with the sound of everything settled happening
here the page resonant & strange
these marks make no sound nothing
that is not is not heard

this moment
this silence
is it clear

an instant
opening to
a music

of sorts now
& not now
offering

nothing
but what
it is

that all is
inevitable accident
a line left
(one of many)

dangling nothing
fails yet   yet

there is no light
& nothing easy
but failure

a moment
in all that is
a whole

to rise
no more

everything slows so
here where time allows
change predominates

age we linger now
go like this sing it
it is no matter

ever laid out in
the world & this
is all we know

old & weary but not yet
torn & so it falls
to us fools as we are

to mend that which
we need hold
to hold us here

wait
the words will come

air audible tonight
dark resonates
& rain

(sing it)
attend there is
no final reason

outside
the bare trees
latent

wait
the leaves will come

that there must be something
because there is
there is this world

& this is what we can know
& what we can do
in this certain darkness
we are eating the world
that is our only home

an indifferent rain
does what it must
& there is nothing new to say
& say it anyway

wake to the sound of water
the sound of plastic in the rain

the earth cannot hold
the water   the air cannot hold
& we would need
we need

that which is difficult to attend
which is love

blue tits feed in the garden
the ground saturated
the air alive

patterns of air
we make
without meaning

the great wheel
turns   we turn

to nothing more
than all we are

here where words
are dislocated
words come
the sun comes too

below the hill the sea
on the hill the trees
a breeze the sea shimmers
heat trembles

the air sing it
quietly to not disturb
the fabric of what is

burn it all
burn waste rubber plastic
anything burn the air
there's money in it

burn your neighbours their children
their cats dogs houses
burn water burn food burn
the soil it grows in burn
there's money in it

burn the grass trees cattle
in the fields burn the very earth
burn the future who needs it
burn it all again burn the money in it

words fail
under the stress
of silence

silence fails
(wait now)
the song avails

of all this failure
forms suppressed
light endures

all that it can
flaring out
to where we are

nothing persists
that remains
unchanging

these lines fall
as they will
in unintended patterns

the lines lie
that nothing is
if it is not
made new

Away

there's a bird
in a tree
in the garden

a small tree
in a small garden

it's a robin
(of course)

& there are other birds
in other trees
in other gardens

it's a willow
a white willow

beyond an oak
alive with blackbirds
nothing but sound

the world is still in the grass
the many grasses

is never simple
was never simple

follow
a single strand
& everything flows.

everything is
that is
& we await

the next
glacial maximum

a road
runs through it
not done not

random a weave
listen: responsibilities

begin in life
the world as is
the bees

the bees are
dying
in the sun
in the stream

in dreams begin
this slow descent
to politics

terrible
terrible

(go now)

of my heart
of my art

slouching
dropping

slow now
the rain
(remember)

it flows
so much waste
against the wind

raise it
raise the pole
draw & listen

to no sound
no breath

twice the rain
over the trees
water above
wood below

fire on the mountain
& on the earth
fire the great
river burning

water goes
its way is not
(the mountain
also flows)

is not
contained
it fills the flaws
the hollow places

rises the ice
melts the mountain
moves time

is not fixed
it burns
attend

we move apart
a part
leaving
the rooted earth

drift   erode
& without shame
appropriate

bird in the air
air on the wing
away   away
nothing agrees
but the wind

out of the light
the wind
& a single rose

the trees
are burning
under heaven
which is not

but sky & air
a line of sparrows
on the low roof
& it is autumn

& all that follows
fire on the water
a mutual need
small things matter

chance arise
small matters
drift but not
apart   a part

willow alive
with sparrows
save us
these small things

sing them
lake still fire still
as need   needs
& we are lost

even the air
cannot redeem
even the oak
ash   willow

away unnamed
rises / the flame
subsides / the wave
what was the question
unanswereds

sun on the water
on the sand
this September
summer

& oh such light
such air
such water
do nothing   sit

50 years considering
words their relations
abandoned that which
must be said

or sung it is not
the order of things
not grasped   dissolves
& oh so light

& it is not
our world
<u>not</u>
we just live here
tenants

in this time
of extinctions

the birds are dying
the bees are dying
the words are dying
& these are not words
& words matter

less than matter
not ours not
dominion
& we are dying

& we take it
anyway

from the fire
the wind
air rises

(a lifetime spent
trying to find
the proper question)

acorns everywhere
 half-eaten   whole
green/brown/shades between

from the wind
they fall
& from the birds
renewed   sessile
immanent

& the cloud
        (stratus)
the grey
& the less grey
rise
& the rain
for clarity

the air crystal
the gravel glazed
& lucid wet
each stone itself
a small thing

the wind moves
the rain moves
the stones

a fair field full
the fairest
the fullest
the wettest

a bare field
air over all
the ruined trees

the use of land
is not just
a need

it is
a harmony
disrupted squeeze
the margins

a bleeding canker
rots us all

the core
disintegrates

& we
stand still

stand
still
an autumn
rises

& still
away   clear
the earth is
that it is

name it
it is not
listen
it is not

change
is the process
the sea
rises

the earth
not

& we must
if we would

lie on the grass
a pillow

these small
matters

diligence
perseverance
caution

water
fire

an end

long poem with no name

if everything to be said
has been said

everything written

if the book is closed

wait
there is work to be done
to recover
that which is spoilt
 to find again
the immanent word
still as night
the storm impending
zoon phonanta
within bounds
a single fragment
of darkness

silence
then speech
then silence

the work remains
a dance of sorts

ludic
& ludicrous
this warm reach
between sand & stone
water   its slow fall

& swell   the drag
of syntax
each wave in its place
in its time

that the world
doesn't need us

that we
need the world

the sound   smell
weave of it
lost here now
in transient words
necessary words
turn of the year
murmuration settle

& sing
in isolation
in chorus
in the space between
tzee tzee tzee tic tic-tic

& silence
again
in the garden
beyond reason
beyond a distant hum
beyond & on
listen

nothing is said
again
tzee tzee tzee
indifferent song

somewhere
ice cracks
somewhere
there is no rain
or too much rain
somewhere
the drift begins
nowhere ends

the cloud
cirrus
deep coral
bleeding
to purple grey

not fire
nor its simulacrum
but water
suspended
in light
we are lost
& have lost

unreconciled
somewhere death
deferred
a seed peels open

unfurls
cells replicate
somewhere a leaf
expresses

nothing said
root & stem
& water
always water

or its absence
the cell's scale
& the star's rhythm
approximate

the world itself
sings itself
singing the world
in apricity

& it is difficult
being here
tic
[singing]
in such stillness

a slow
extraction
web of effects
& interactions
bole & leaf

a system
alive
thunder
then rain
a release of sorts

there is no normal
no new
& no return
but the bud sets
the leaf inheres

rises
the rain the lake
the sea
an absence of
restraint

we rest on what
is not the case
is not
a continuity
disrupted

a single robin
singing
defiance

rain &
the water rises
inexorably
everything flows

that is
this fragile world

a quiet grave
in a quiet time

seamounts scarred
& littered
but alive
precariously
alive

a system the earth
is not our mother
it is indifferent
& is not ours
not a commodity
it is an it
it is
where we live

it will survive us
despite us

it will outlast
our plastic
(enduring monument)
it will outlast
what we call life

in the nature
of nature
nothing happens

but language
gets us nowhere
the karst
doesn't care
nor the chert

the fluorspar
endures

no end
only endings
an accretion of
links   connections
the weave of things

bluntly
we're not killing
the earth

amongst the rest
we're killing ourselves

speak now
the lakes provide
& persevere
& there is joy
despite it all
(remember)

a single butterfly
(small tortoise shell)
in September sun
descending

the breeze stirs
& the mountains move
as they must

somewhere
a crack widens
water rises

roof bends
& walls break
a house disrupted

each breath
a new life
a new dying
rest now

the necessary words
an absence
of silence

— . —

that it is spring
(the first day of spring)
& that it rains
& that you are dead

robins nest
in the bay

no tits
(this year)
in the box

blackbirds
above
in the oaks

each in its time
the low hum of life

leaves fall
& sap rises
(a cycle)

& there are limits
& limitations

rain:
the lake fills
and floods

the 5th direction
is where you are
where you would be

& the work
remains undone

undone
this cold spring
this wet spring
sing nothing

await the sun

Coda

Ms Moore's Menagerie

No words so fine as your
    literal
imagination lures
    – vital–
from this everyday
    biddable
world of cliché

as untrammelled dragons
    preserved in
language's clear cocoon
wherein
everything remains –
    our chagrin
cannot distrain

the beast's estate: reptiles
    a small rat
patterns of sound beguile
so that
the genuine finds space
    whereat
to fill our minds

with these your animals
    a garden
of delights – carnivals –
Arden
or ardent never
    harden
nor dissever

Ms Moore your careful words
    bring pleasure
real or imagined birds
measured
in their concision
    a treasure
of provision.

Acknowledgements

Sections from 'Four' were published in *Uimhir a Cúig*, Feb 2017 and *otata 24*, December 2017 and *The Stinging Fly*, May 2022. The whole text was set as a cantata by David Bremner and performed by ensembÉal in Christchurch Cathedral, Dublin on 9th November, 2018.

Sections from 'Uncertain Songs' were included in *Icarus* Summer 2017 issue and *FourXFour 28*, Spring 2019. The following note was published with the *Icarus* selection:

> These texts are from a work in progress called, unsurprisingly enough, *Uncertain Songs*. In writing them, I have two things partly in mind. One is Thomas Wyatt's *Certain Psalms of David*, written when that kind of certainty was more readily available. It is my view that uncertainty is a preferable condition. The other is the following quotation from the Postface to Charles Ives' *114 Songs* of 1922:

> *Some of the songs in this book, particularly among the latter ones, cannot be sung, and if they could, perhaps might prefer, if they had a say, to remain as they are; that is, "in the leaf" and that they will remain in this peaceful state is more than presumable.*

'Ms Moore's Menagerie' was published by Rupert Loydell's *Stride* magazine as 'MM's Menagerie'.

My thanks to all concerned.

Biography

Billy Mills was born Dublin in 1954. After some years spent in Spain and the UK, he currently lives in Limerick. He is co-editor (with Catherine Walsh) of hardpressed Poetry. His *Lares/Manes: Collected Poems* was published by Shearsman Books in 2009, and *Imaginary Gardens* and *Loop Walks* by hardPressed poetry in 2012 and 2013 respectively. Most recently, *The City Itself* was published by Hesterglock Press in 2017.

Milton Keynes UK
Ingram Content Group UK Ltd.
UKHW020237300924
448889UK00001B/9